CUSTOMER SERVICE EXCELLENCE   **Libraries & Archives**

Kent
County
Council

Make Your Own Art

Painting

FRANKLIN WATTS
LONDON•SYDNEY

First published in 2008 by Franklin Watts

© 2008 Arcturus Publishing Limited

Franklin Watts
338 Euston Road
London NW1 3BH

Franklin Watts Australia
Level 17/207 Kent Street, Sydney, NSW 2000

Produced by Arcturus Publishing Limited,
26/27 Bickels Yard, 151–153 Bermondsey Street,
London SE1 3HA

Editor: Alex Woolf
Designers: Sally Henry and Trevor Cook
Consultant: Daisy Fearns

Picture credits: Sally Henry and Trevor Cook

Every attempt has been made to clear copyright.
Should there be any inadvertent omission,
please apply to the publisher for rectification.

A CIP catalogue record for this book is available
from the British Library.

Dewey Decimal Classification Number: 750

ISBN 978 0 7496 8191 3

Printed in China

Franklin Watts is a division of Hachette Children's Books,
an Hachette Livre UK company.
www.hachettelivre.co.uks.

Contents

Introduction

This book contains a variety of projects to help develop your skills at painting. You can begin with something observed or completely imaginary. The object is to produce something that you can be proud of and be pleased to keep and display.

Paper

We usually paint on white or coloured paper or card. Most of the projects in this book have been done on **cartridge paper**. This is a strong kind of paper that can be used for drawing or painting. One advantage of paper over heavier materials is that you can easily trim your picture to the best shape and size when you've finished.

Drawing board

You will need something to support your paper while you work. Your paper may come in a pad, which may have a stiff back, but using a drawing board is much better. A piece of plywood about 600 x 400 mm (24 x 16 in) will do. Make sure it's flat. This is big enough for an **A3-size** piece of paper, 297 x 420 mm (11.75 x 16.5 in). Use sticky tape to hold the paper in place on the board. Leaving a margin unpainted around your painting will help it to stay flat. You can cut out your painting when you've finished.

Paint

We've used **poster paints** and **ready-mixed paints** in the projects in the book. They can be used thick or thin and colours can be mixed. You can make the paint thinner by adding water. You can buy various pots and mixing palettes. We like mixing our paint on old white plates, and having water in yogurt pots!

Brushes

Brushes can be expensive, so it's very important to try as many as you can before you buy your own. In the instructions we suggest some ideal sizes, but mostly you are going to need one brush for painting large areas of colour, and another for detail work. Soft brushes are best with the paint we are going to use.

round brushes

Some brushes are designed for special jobs. You might find you like using them in your painting. The **lettering brush** is designed for drawing letters neatly, but it also makes some interesting marks. The **blending brush** is used dry to blend areas of wet colour into each other.

flat brush

blending brush

lettering brush

Colour

It's possible to get quite good results with just a few basic colours. Here's a group of colours mixed from only six pots of colour – magenta, yellow, cyan, red, green and blue. Keep your paints clean when you mix colours. Always wash your brush when you change colours.

Adding white to your colour makes a **tint**.

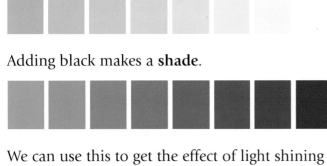

Adding black makes a **shade**.

We can use this to get the effect of light shining on something.

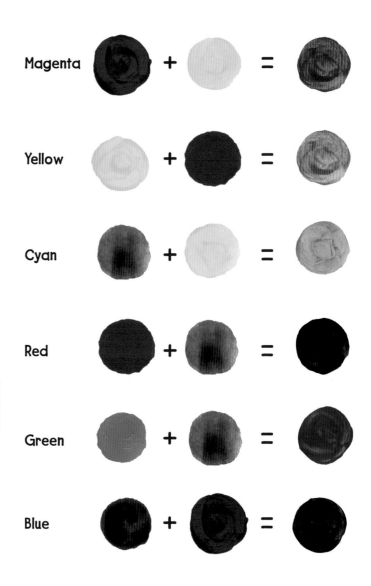

Magenta + =

Yellow + =

Cyan + =

Red + =

Green + =

Blue + =

Aerial perspective

When we look into the distance, especially when there is moisture in the air, colours appear paler and more blue the further away they are. This is useful to show depth in a landscape.

Linear perspective

Where there are straight lines in the landscape, such as buildings, roads or railway tracks, following a few simple rules will help your picture to be more realistic. Make a vanishing point in your picture. Things going directly away from you will disappear into the distance at this point.

Framing the view

Make one of these handy devices to help you compose your picture.

• A piece of stout card with an oblong hole in it about 180 x 130mm (7 x 5in).

Tracing

If you've copied a picture by tracing it using tracing paper, you might need to transfer the drawing to another piece of paper. Turn the tracing over and rub soft pencil over where the drawing is. Place the tracing, right way up, on the new paper and draw over all the lines. This will transfer the drawing onto the paper.

Looking after your work

Always take care of your work. Finishing your painting session and clearing away must include making your work safe for the next session, or preserving your finished paintings. Keep your flat artwork in a folder – you can easily make one from two sheets of stout cardboard and some duct tape, like the one on the right.

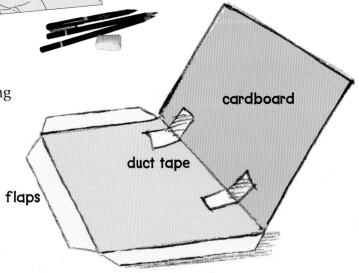

cardboard

duct tape

flaps

Self-portrait

Painting a good SELF-PORTRAIT is a skill that takes lots of practice. Let's be our own model!

45 MINUTES

10 MINUTES

You will need:

- *Cartridge paper*
- *Paints and mixing palette*
- *Brushes, round 3, 6 and flat 12mm (0.125, 0.25 and 0.5 in)*
- *Wall or table mirror*
- *Chair or stool*

What to do...

Make sure your mirror is firmly fixed and in the right place. Sit in front of the mirror with your board so you can comfortably see both your reflection and your drawing without moving your head. Is there enough light?

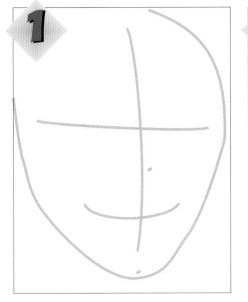

Lightly draw the shape of your head. Halfway down, draw a guideline for your eyes, then one for your mouth. Put in a centre line. Put dots for the tip of your nose and your chin.

Mix up some thick paint to make a skin colour. Using a 6mm (0.25in) brush, paint in the shapes of your eyes, mouth, nose, face and neck. Look very carefully at your eyes in the mirror.

Using your small brush, paint in your eye colour. Put black dots in the centre for the pupils. A tiny white highlight dot will make your eyes look more lifelike.

Model your skin colour in three shades. Touch in your lips, then use a bigger brush to paint your hair. Add hair colours: dark first, then texture with lighter colours.

Add detail to your mouth and teeth. Use dark hair colour for eyebrows and eyelashes. Be careful – you can change your expression with these!

Check details … tidy up. Well done – it's finished!

Simple still life

Painters through the ages have used STILL LIFE to show off lots of different ways of painting. Here we are using it to explore colour.

35 MINUTES

10 MINUTES

You will need:

- *Cartridge paper*
- *Soft pencil, ruler*
- *Paints, mixing palette and water*
- *Brushes, 6, 12 and 25mm (0.125, 0.25 and 0.5 in)*
- *Objects to make an arrangement*

What to do...

Set up your group of objects in a good light. We've chosen plain backgrounds and strong colours for our first still life. Use your viewfinder frame to check your composition. Place your paper so that you can work and look directly at your group of objects. Draw a large square on your paper in pencil to mark out the shape of your painting.

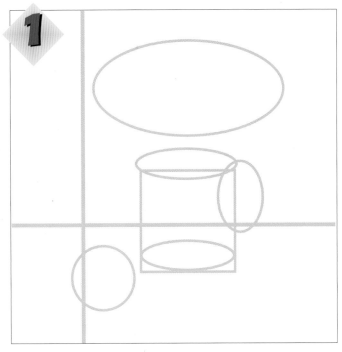

Our composition seems to fit well on a square shape. Place the objects in the painting using simple outlines only.

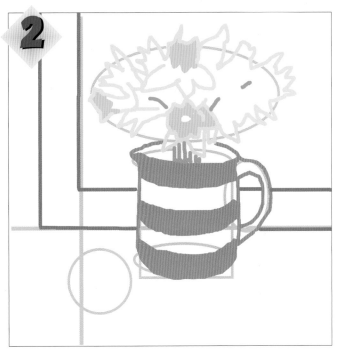

We are using the edges of our window to make a big L-shape in the background. It helps to frame our arrangement. Next, we sketch in the flowers and the jug.

This picture is all flat shapes, but we can use the outline to describe the different things in it. Paint the table, wall and window with flat colours.

Keep your edges crisp and colours clear. A little extra detail added to the flowers among all the flat shapes gives the picture focus.

My own room

45 MINUTES

10 MINUTES

12

When you make a painting of your OWN ROOM, you're free to put in all the things that are important to you, and to leave out everything that's dull and boring. If you want to change the decor, here's a way of trying new colour schemes without making a big mess!

You will need:

- *Cartridge paper, soft pencil*
- *Ruler*
- *Paints, mixing palette and water*
- *Brushes, 6, 12 and 25mm*
  (0.125, 0.25 and 0.5 in)

What to do...

Think about the shape of your room. What would you see if you took away one wall and looked inside? First, draw the box shape you'd have if there wasn't any furniture in the room at all.

Outline three or four of the important things in your room. We chose the bed, the chest of drawers, the rug and the picture.

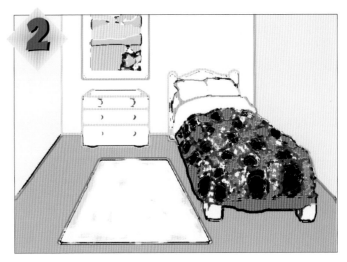

In your painting, try putting different colours on the walls, floor and ceiling.

Notice how strong colours change the room. Dark walls can make the room feel smaller.

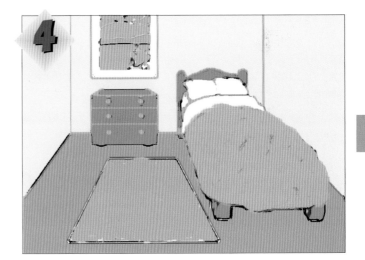

Light-coloured walls can make your room seem bigger.

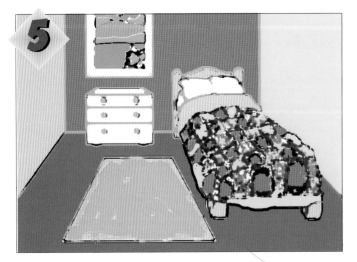

Reds and yellows make the room feel warmer.

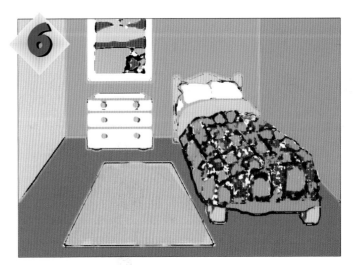

Greens and blues give the room a colder feel.

Landscape

40 MINUTES

10 MINUTES

14

LANDSCAPE is all about what you can see outdoors, but that doesn't have to mean the countryside. A town or city view can be just as interesting to a painter. You can find natural scenes to paint in parks and gardens.

You will need:

- Card or paper, tissues
- Paint, mixing palette and water
- Brushes, round 3, 6 and flat 12mm (0.125, 0.25 and 0.5 in)
- Card to make a framing window

What to do...

Find a view that interests you. You may start from a photograph, but it's often more interesting to start with the real thing. You can choose a viewpoint you really like. Use the framing window to find a good composition in the landscape. We chose our view for its bright colours and surprising patterns.

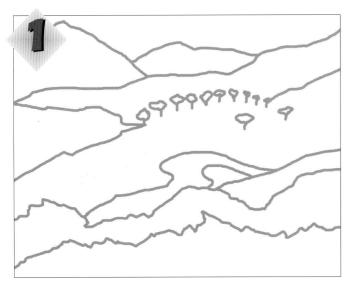

Look carefully at your composition. Try to see the pattern in the landscape. Sometimes it helps to screw up your eyes to blur the view so you can't see detail. Outline the patches of colour with light grey paint and a fine brush. Put in key details such as trees.

Start filling in the shapes. Do the light colours first. Don't worry about painting over your drawing lines. You can give a feeling of depth by making colours more washed out towards the horizon. Build up the trees and bushes with light and dark greens.

Use light blue to create the sky. Add darker blue as required. If your sky has clouds, you can leave the paper unpainted to show up as white shapes. Paint landscapes in settled weather conditions to avoid the light changing.

Our picture was done in the early evening when the hills looked very pink. Add darker colours last, to show shadows under trees, for example. Make a note of where and when you made the painting.

Dinosaur

Use a toy dinosaur for a model. Get up close to one of nature's most terrifying beasts.

You will need:

- *Model dinosaur*
- *Pencil, coloured markers*
- *Drawing paper*
- *Paints, brushes and water*

20
MINUTES

What to do...

Position your model dinosaur against a plain background. We used a T-Rex, but you can use any models you have at home.

5
MINUTES

Here is a photo of our model. There's lots of detail. We can choose which bits to paint.

Make a pencil drawing of the head. Check the angle by looking at your model. Draw in his teeth, then carefully position his eye.

Use a black marker to draw over your pencil lines and make textures.

Use paint to fill in the background areas. We used blues and greens for the land, but try out wild colours in your paintings. It's great fun!

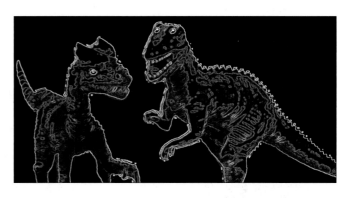

Figure painting

35 MINUTES

10 MINUTES

18

Painting figures takes lots of practice. To help you develop your skills, first try using a photograph as a basis for your painting. You may find that you need to research details like hands by looking at real ones.

You will need:

- *Card or paper, tracing paper*
- *Drawing board, soft pencil*
- *Tape or drawing pins, tissues*
- *Paints, mixing palette and water*
- *Brushes, round 3, 6 and flat 12mm (0.125, 0.25 and 0.5 in)*

What to do...

Try to find a large photograph to make a tracing for a same-size painting. Otherwise you could scale up your picture as described on page 26. On page 22 we help you draw from a live model.

Select the part of the picture you want to use. Here we are going to leave out the boy on the right.

Tape tracing paper over the photo and make a detailed line drawing in pencil. Take care to include as much detail as you can.

Cover the back of the tracing with soft pencil. Transfer the image to your drawing paper.

Using paint mixed with lots of water, lay pale colour washes over your drawing.

Study your photo to find more details to add.

Paint in shadows, skin tones and more detail.

Creatures

All sorts of CREATURES bring colour into our world. Let's celebrate our favourite animal by making a painting.

35 MINUTES

10 MINUTES

You will need:

- *Cartridge paper or thin card*
- *Paper varnish*
- *Black marker pens, soft pencil*
- *Paint, mixing palette and water*
- *Brushes, round 3, 6 and flat 12mm (0.125, 0.25 and 0.5 in)*
- *Magazines, scissors*

What to do...

Find a photograph of an animal or bird that you can draw on. For our picture, we've chosen to paint just the macaw's head and body. We are using the top half of our photo. You can trim your reference picture to improve the design for your painting. Draw a grid of squares on your photo.

1

Our photo divides neatly into four units one way and three units the other.

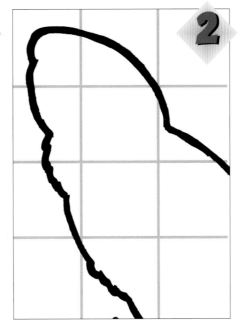

2

On the painting paper, draw similar squares, but they can be bigger to fit the paper. Now we can start drawing. Begin with the outline. The grid helps to

3

place it accurately. Next, use a finer pen to draw in all the smaller shapes. Be careful to get the eye in the right place.

4

Once you have drawn round all the different coloured feathers, you can start colouring them.

5

If your model is brightly coloured like our parrot, you need to keep your colours clear and bright, too! Finish off with some clear paper varnish.

If you have a pet...

Make a big drawing in marker pen, then paint it!

Pop art posters

55 MINUTES

5 MINUTES

Portraits are often painted in realistic colours, but you can go wild! See what you can do!

You will need:

- *Card, paper, tracing paper, tissues*
- *Black marker pens, soft pencil, photocopier*
- *Magazine pictures or a photograph*
- *Black wax crayon, paints, brushes and water*

What to do...

You could work with a model for this project. Otherwise use a photo or magazine picture. Try to get A3-size photocopies to paint. The four pictures together will be very impressive.

Make a line drawing or tracing from a good photograph.

Outline the features, hair and some details of clothing.

Make four big photocopies and paint in the areas with colour.

23

Purple, orange and green are unlikely, but interesting!

Blue, green and purple are cool colours.

Green, yellow and pink gives an unearthly complexion!

24

Make a line drawing from a photograph or from a model. Transfer your drawing to four separate sheets of paper by tracing down (see page 7) or by using a photocopier.

Use a black wax crayon to draw over the outlines on each copy. Try to follow your original lines, but don't worry if they are not all the same.

Colour the four pictures differently, as on page 24. The wax crayon will resist the paint and make it easy to colour in. Differences in the drawings will add interest.

These are some of the warm colours we used.

House of wax

Painting buildings is quite a challenge. We've chosen to paint one looking straight on, with plenty of detail but without very much depth. We have scaled-up the drawing from a small reference picture and used a wax resist effect on dark paper. Are you ready to have a go?

You will need:

40 MINUTES

- Dark-coloured paper
- Drawing pad or board
- Tape or drawing pins, tissues
- White pencil, ruler
- Paints and mixing palette
- Brushes, round 3, 6 and 12mm (0.125, 0.25 and 0.5 in)
- Photocopy of reference picture
- Wax candle
- Washing-up liquid

What to do...

10 MINUTES

Use a photocopy of your picture. Fix your dark paper to your drawing board. Follow the steps to create the grids. Move from square to square transferring the main structure lines from the reference to your work. Experiment with wax and paint mixed with ordinary washing-up liquid to get great texture effects.

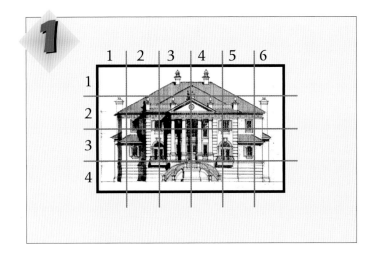

Use a photocopy reference smaller than your work. Draw a grid of squares on the reference.

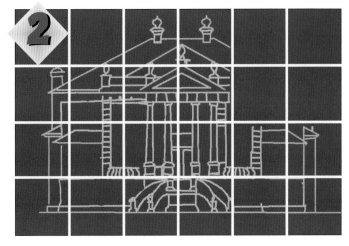

Draw the same number of squares, but larger, on your paper. Draw lightly in white pencil.

In each square, copy the outlines in grey paint. When dry, draw over the outlines with a candle.

Paint your house with thinned paint. The colour should run off the waxy lines.

27

Mixing washing-up liquid with your paint produces interesting effects.

We've filled in the sky with blue, but you can leave it as dark paper colour if you prefer.

Magic palace

We've painted an imaginary palace, full of colour, with an exotic garden. Follow our way of building up a painting or create your own in a similar way.

The MAGIC PALACE is a painting full of busy patterns. Look at the enlarged details in colour. We have made simple line drawings of the patterns.

Before you start your own magic palace, try drawing some patterns in line. Paint them in with colours you

like. This is the time to experiment. When you find a set of colours that look good together,

keep them for your next painting.

To add to the textures, we have often painted over dry colour with more detail. You can do this too. We also

used a fine metallic gold marker to outline some parts of the

painting. It gives it a really rich result. By freely experimenting, you can create your own effects.

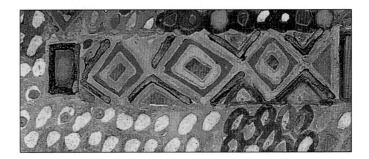

Plan your painting by doing a line drawing of your palace.

Using another colour, draw in some plants in the garden and some people.

Paint in the background of the painting. Use flat colours to fill in the shapes you've drawn.

Add further interest to the picture by putting in more and more detail and texture. It's good fun.

Glossary

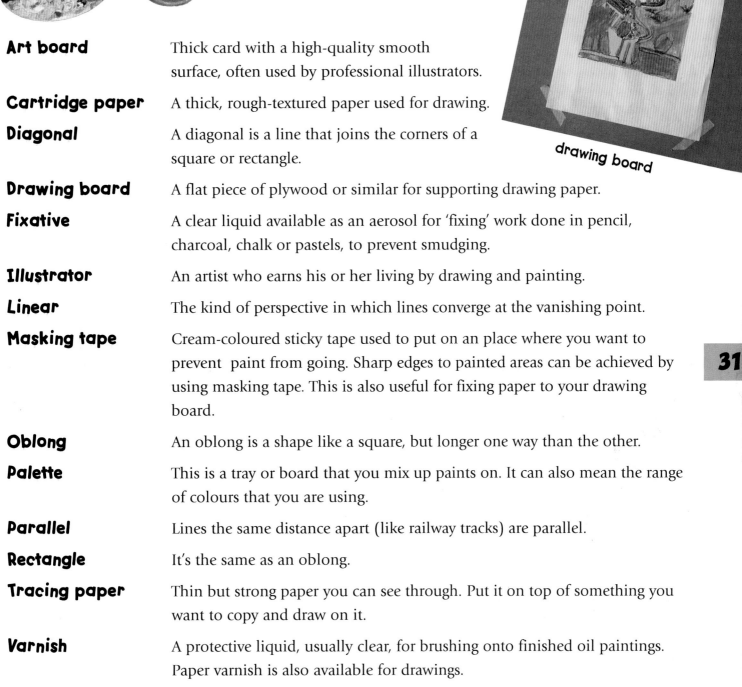

drawing board

Art board Thick card with a high-quality smooth surface, often used by professional illustrators.

Cartridge paper A thick, rough-textured paper used for drawing.

Diagonal A diagonal is a line that joins the corners of a square or rectangle.

Drawing board A flat piece of plywood or similar for supporting drawing paper.

Fixative A clear liquid available as an aerosol for 'fixing' work done in pencil, charcoal, chalk or pastels, to prevent smudging.

Illustrator An artist who earns his or her living by drawing and painting.

Linear The kind of perspective in which lines converge at the vanishing point.

Masking tape Cream-coloured sticky tape used to put on an place where you want to prevent paint from going. Sharp edges to painted areas can be achieved by using masking tape. This is also useful for fixing paper to your drawing board.

Oblong An oblong is a shape like a square, but longer one way than the other.

Palette This is a tray or board that you mix up paints on. It can also mean the range of colours that you are using.

Parallel Lines the same distance apart (like railway tracks) are parallel.

Rectangle It's the same as an oblong.

Tracing paper Thin but strong paper you can see through. Put it on top of something you want to copy and draw on it.

Varnish A protective liquid, usually clear, for brushing onto finished oil paintings. Paper varnish is also available for drawings.

Index